T0077998

STUFF HAPPENS

(A Lifetime of Coincidents)

Jack Tep

authorHOUSE

AuthorHouse™
1663 Liberty Drive
Bloomington, IN 47403
www.authorhouse.com
Phone: 833-262-8899

Published by AuthorHouse 04/21/2022

ISBN: 978-1-6655-5747-4 (sc)
ISBN: 978-1-6655-5746-7 (e)

Library of Congress Control Number: 2022907572

Print information available on the last page.

In Memory Of
OUR BELOVED

COREEN ELIZABETH

Born July 4, 1963

Died February 21, 2007

At the age of forty-three cancer took her life. She will
be in our hearts and remembered forever

Introduction

The music, movies, and numerous other bits of popular culture mentioned in this book were never really about my life. But somehow, from time to time, they just fit it like a glove. Just as some of them may have done for you in your own lives. Or just as some completely different slices of the changing cultural scene—perhaps "Satin Doll" or another beautiful Duke Ellington tune voiced by the guitar of Joe Pass, or the outsider's lament of Boy George singing the title song of the movie called The Crying Game—may have done for people of other generations than my own.

The point is this one of a kind book playfully explores specific moments in my life when either coincidence or chance delivered songs, movies, fads, and turns of history that resonated strongly for me and for people around me. Those things weren't about me, and I certainly didn't cause them to happen. But they did happen, and they did form part of the sound track of my life, reflecting key moments in both my personal history and the much bigger world around all of us. I hope you'll enjoy experiencing these meaningful echoes, and in that process, you will reflect on the many funny ways that the culture around us can mirror our own life and time.

Aunt Sally was a performer and ice skater at the Roxy Theater in New York City. She performed with Sonja Henie productions in the 1940's. Henie was an ice skater from Oslo, Norway. In addition to being as cute as a button, she won three gold medals in the Olympic Games—along with many other skating triumphs around the world. Henie parlayed her success into quite a show business career, including costarring in Hollywood films with such big names as Don Ameche and Tyrone Power. She also put on many productions at the Roxy Theater in Manhattan, which is where aunt Sally comes in.

While working as a performer, Aunt Sally met a fellow by the name of Raymond Lee. They met in the early 1950s at a bar called Jilly's on the west side of Manhattan. Jilly's was also frequented by the "Chairman of the Board," Frank Sinatra. Raymond was the actual "chairman of the board" and president of Lockport Felt Co. and a few years after Lockport Felt was sold to Carborundum Corporation, Raymond became chairman of the Power Company of the state of New York. He and Sally married in the mid nineteen-fifties. It wasn't long after that when the Bobbettes, an all-girl vocal group from Spanish Harlem, had a big 1957 hit with their song "Mr. Lee."

In the early 1960s, Raymond was appointed by New York Governor Nelson Rockefeller to be the Sports Commissioner for the state of New York. He held that post for almost ten years before resigning. When Nelson Rockefeller resigned his governorship in

1974 in order to accept his appointment for the Vice Presidency with the Gerald Ford administration, Rockefeller's lieutenant governor, Malcolm Wilson, became governor of New York State. It was then that Governor Wilson appointed Raymond as Chairman of the Power Company of New York State.

Ten years earlier, in 1964, Senator Barry Goldwater of Arizona ran for president and chose a representative from New York to be his running mate. Bill Miller was a lawyer from Lockport, New York and chairman of the Republican Party from the early sixties to when he was selected as Goldwater's running mate. Miller was also Raymond's lawyer and good friend. Whenever Miller held a press conference, it was at Raymond's house. My father, John, had the privilege of travelling around the country with the presidential hopeful.

In the mid-seventies, Sally and Raymond built a house in Southern California. The house was built into a mountain and the front of the house was built of glass from top to bottom. The house was in Pauma Valley, a gorgeous community that lies north by northeast from San Diego. In the valley was a golf course. The view was spectacular and was surrounded by avocado orchards. Just a short time after they moved into the house, I became aware of the popular saying, "People who live in glass houses shouldn't throw stones."

I was invited to visit them in Pauma Valley. One day, aunt Sally suggested that we take a day trip to Mount Palomar, home of the world- famous planetary observatory. It took close to an hour to get there. When we departed the valley, temperatures were in the seventies. As we travelled to Palomar mountain we could see people jumping off cliffs and hang gliding to the bottom. As we continued driving and were navigating our way up Mt Palomar, it was getting colder and when we arrived at the top it was remarkably cold, and there were two-foot snow banks shoveled to the side of the road.

It was also a road with many curves as we climbed to the top. There were no guardrails, and the journey became rather scary. On top of the mountain was the observatory, which was managed by Caltech. There we enjoyed a description of galaxies far up in the sky; their distances from us were measured in light years. We stayed for a short period of time before travelling back to the valley.

Shortly after I returned home to the east coast, the news reported that Princess Grace Kelly, the Philadelphia-born movie star who had married Prince Rainier of Monaco, had rolled her Range Rover over the side of a mountain on the way to Paris where her daughter Stephanie was starting school. They claimed the brakes failed, and she couldn't stop the car.

My real-life Uncle Sam attended Stuyvesant High School in Manhattan in the years prior to World War II. He played football at Stuyvesant, excelling in the sport with his heavily muscled body. Sam joined the army in the early forties and became a decorated veteran of World War II. Whenever he needed a pack of Camel cigarettes, he would walk to the nearby country store which was almost exactly a mile from the farmhouse in which we lived. Around that era, the cigarette commercial "I'd walk a mile for a Camel" was a popular ad on early television broadcasts.

Uncle Sam died in 1960. His funeral was held at St. Patrick's Cathedral in Manhattan, and he was buried at Calvary Cemetery in Queens. It seemed everyone stopped talking about Uncle Sam when "Uncle Sam" died. Maybe the Vietnam era had made us all a bit weary of war.

We had many family members still in New York. My cousin Nancy lived in Commack, Long Island. She lost her husband, remarried, and then moved to Sandy Hook, Connecticut. Due to the problems with her husband's health while she lived in Sandy Hook she eventually packed her family and moved from Sandy Hook to Florida.

Nancy had two granddaughters, one called Ashley and the other Madison. In the year 2015, there was a scandal revolving around a "dating" Web site named Ashley-Madison.

Another branch of our family lived in Astoria, Queens. That was Andy and his wife Ann. The two of them greatly enjoyed traveling, and they owned an apartment house in Astoria, Queens off Broadway. They became known as Raggedy Ann and Raggedy Andy. (Trust me, they weren't raggedy at all).

When I was a young kid, my mother always called me Jackie. In the late forties, when television first became a household item, Jackie Gleason was one of the earliest and biggest stars. He was first on Cavalcade of Stars, and then in the mid fifties, he started The Jackie Gleason Show with characters that became known and loved throughout the country, like the bus driver Ralph Kramden, Joe the Bartender, Reginald Van Gleason III, the Poor Soul, and others.

My brother and I were born in Bronx, New York City and lived on Undercliff Ave. In the late 1940s, we moved from New York to Connecticut. After we moved, it seemed that the Bronx changed forever. We had moved from New York City to Connecticut because my father changed jobs from Curtiss-Wright Aeronautical to United Technologies. He was an engineer and designed many parts for the aircraft industry.

In the sixties, Carol Burnett starred in her own show with Tim Conway and Harvey Korman joining as costars. The show went on for a while and was totally entertaining. I would always see the different shows and never pay much attention to what entertainers were saying. At the end of her show, Carol would tug on her ear, reminding us to listen!

On a sunny afternoon in the summer in the early fifties, after school, I decided to mow the lawn. The lawn had a considerable incline. I pushed the mower up the incline, and on the way down the slope, the mower went over my foot, slicing through my shoe, and cutting my toe pretty seriously. My mother didn't drive, so she called a neighbor. He provided transportation to the hospital where they operated on my foot. The doctor was unable to salvage my toe. I hobbled along for weeks with my foot in a cast and crutches tucked under my arms. Not long after that operation, the television Western hero Hopalong Cassidy appeared, played by William Boyd and based on some popular books from about fifty years earlier. Hopalong, sometimes call Hoppy for short, became one of the most popular television series. And meanwhile, I could be seen hopping along with my crutches for a long time.

The house where we lived was in a rural town called Mansfield. It was soon after we moved that Jayne Mansfield became a Hollywood celebrity. She lost her life in an automobile accident in Louisiana, in 1967, when her car went under the back of a truck in low-visibility conditions. The truck was moving slow and spraying for mosquitoes. As a result of that accident, trailers came to be equipped with "Mansfield bars," protective steel bars that prevent cars from going under them as the result of the rear-end collision.

While we lived in Mansfield, my father bought a beautiful female collie. He then built a doghouse, fenced in an area, and bred "Lassie" the collie. Soon after, there were many little collies running around. It was not long after that when a television series starring a collie called Lassie became popular in the mid-fifties.

During this time, we went on a YMCA-sponsored trip to Boston to watch the Boston Braves baseball team. Within a short period of time of our trip, the Boston Braves moved from Boston to Milwaukee where they became known as the Milwaukee Braves.

In the mid-fifties, I became interested in the game of golf. I picked up a golf club from my father's bag and began swinging it in the backyard. Soon after my introduction to golf, Jack Paar began hosting the Tonight Show. When I applied for a driver's license and passed my test, my father bought me a car. The car was ten years old and was reliable. Then the Tonight Show changed hosts to become The Tonight Show starring Johnny Carson. Johnny hosted the show for thirty years and retired in the early nineties. His signature gesture when he finished his opening monologue was to swing an imaginary golf club. That swing signified that the main part of his popular show was now underway.

While I attended a private school in Connecticut, our family planned a trip to Palisades Park in Palisades, New Jersey. Within a year after that visit, Palisades Park was gone, replaced forever by new condominium buildings in 1971. Of course, the park still lives on in the 1962 hit song "Palisades Park" by Freddie Cannon which was later recut by the Beach Boys, the Ramones, and others.

My friends and I were walking to the movies one Saturday afternoon, and a small cat crossed our path. One of the fellows grabbed the cat and threw it up on a metal awning. There were steps nearby and the cat was not in trouble. We left it there to find its own way down to the sidewalk. A short time after that, in 1958, a movie came out called Cat on a Hot Tin Roof. It was one of Paul Newman's earlier films and also starred Elizabeth Taylor who looked very curvy in the white full-length slip she wore for much of the movie. Burl Ives, who co-starred as Big Daddy, was curvy too—but more like a beach ball than an hourglass.

My father always told me to be a non-conformist, not to be afraid, to be different from others, and to make my own individual choices. Suddenly, the Lone Ranger became one of the most popular television series of the fifties, and then the ultimate nonconformist hero, James Dean, starred with Natalie Wood in a 1955 movie called Rebel without a Cause. He instantly became the symbol of restless misunderstood American youth.

While in the eighth grade, I attended a dance. However, this was my first dance, and I did not know how to function out on the dance floor. A friend of mine by the name of Eddie came along and took me to another room and instructed me on a few dance steps. It was soon after that, in 1956, that a song named "Eddie My Love" became popular. The Teen Queens, a girl group, had a big hit with "Eddie" which was in a languid doo-wop style and was later copied by the Chordettes and others.

My father played the violin while the family lived in a Manhattan tenement. His sisters would always complain when he practiced, so to keep peace, he went up on the roof to practice. Then in 1964, along came the now-classic musical about Russian Jewish life, Fiddler on the Roof. It won nine Tony Awards and became the first show in Broadway history to exceed three thousand performances. For nearly ten years, it remained the most performed musical ever, and it also became a very popular 1971 movie.

My grandparents bought a farm in Connecticut that was about a hundred acres in size. There were pigs for slaughter, cows for milking and eating, chickens for laying eggs and roasting. When we needed food for the evening dinner, my grandmother would go to the henhouse, grab a chicken, and cut the head off. Blood would go flying. It was during the farm era that a drink called "Bloody Mary," made with vodka and tomato juice, became popular. Of course, my grandmother's name happened to be Mary. We also had a rooster who would crow every morning and wake everyone up. It didn't take much time for that rooster to be roasted.

There was also a pond where ducks and geese would gather. All these animals had names inspired by George Orwell's book Animal Farm.

The farm was self-sufficient, and on weekends in the summer, my grandmother and I would go out and pick blueberries. Around that time, Fats Domino had a tremendous hit with an old song called "Blueberry Hill." To us kids, it was the newest thing, an instant classic of 1956 with an irresistible New Orleans groove like an undertow. But older and wiser heads recognized the tune from a while back when it had a different title.

Also in 1956, my father bought one of the swankiest and most conservative-looking cars then on the market, a brand-new Packard Patrician. Among its many luxury features was a torsion-bar suspension which, when switched on, would level out the car to compensate for changes in weight distribution such as a heavy load in the trunk or in the backseat.

In those days, because of the hot rodding style with different cars racing around an oval and trends that mimicked the California dry-lake race cars with their back ends elevated high to facilitate changing differential gears, the coolest thing was to have your car lowered in the front but up high in the back. This was called a "California Rake."

One day my friends and I took the Patrician out for a ride. We stopped in a parking lot, and we all sat on top of the trunk. The torsion-bar suspension responded by producing an upward push. As we climbed off the trunk, the car's rear-end went up in the air. It was then that we turned the tortion bar off and the car remained in that position. We rode around the rest of the afternoon with the costliest car in town and before long everyone could be seen featuring a California Rake.

While we were in the eighth grade, my friend Larry and I went to New York City. We didn't have great financial resources, and we stayed at a not-too-expensive hotel. We hid our money and whatever valuables under the mattress and went out sightseeing. Soon after our visit to New York City, Elvis Presley was singing a song about "Heartbreak Hotel."

When we were about to graduate grammar school, the school playground was leveled and paved. Pretty soon, along came the movie Asphalt Jungle, a drama about juvenile delinquents, starring Glenn Ford and powered by a sound track that featured Bill Haley and the Comets doing "Rock Around the Clock," a song that began a nice run of hits for the band. Their sound, like Elvis's, was a jumpy collision of blues and country music that everyone called "rock and roll".

It was at the same period that on New Year's Eve my friend and I mixed some whiskey and scotch from home and did our own celebrating. The police caught up with us, and I was taken and detained at the local police station. Larry's uncle was a prominent physician in town, and he did not get to appear at the police station under those scandalous circumstances. It was a short while after that when Elvis rose up the charts with a song called "Jailhouse Rock." It was written by Jerry Lieber and Mike Stoller, two music-loving Jewish kids from New York who didn't meet until their teenage years, after both of their families had moved to California. They became two of the most popular songwriters of the fifties and sixties with hits like "Under the Boardwalk," "Stand By Me," and "Three Cool Cats."

I always enjoyed going to the YMCA. We would go to the gym and play ball or play ping pong in the recreation area. One summer in the late fifties, I found myself on a bus headed for New York City and stayed at the YMCA in Manhattan. After a couple of days, I found a bus heading back to Connecticut and returned home. It was a short time after staying at the "Y" in New York City that the Village People sang their popular hit called "YMCA."

In 1959, a girl by the name of Phyllis Monroe appeared on the scene. We were in the senior year of high school, and we kind of hit it off. Shortly after, in 1961, Elvis released a slow romantic ballad called "Can't Help Falling in Love with You." Phyllis And I continued our "on again, off again relationship". When I look back it seems that when It was the "off again" part of our affair that was the most dangerous. The song "Me and Mrs. Jones sums it up quite well.

While in school, I was the president of a youth group. At one time we were riding in the backseat of a car with a group of four other fellows who got it into their heads to break into a liquor store. Another fellow and I sat in the backseat asking why we were parked in a parking lot near the liquor store or why we even there. We had no idea of what was happening. The two fellows in the front left the car broke a window and entered the store. After being waved to come in, we got out of the car and entered the store through the broken window. A few weeks later, I was arrested. The state police wrote out a statement, and I signed it. Although I was only fifteen at the time there was no support.

It was then that I had to resign as president of the youth group and this episode changed my life forever. No one else was held responsible for the break-in. Thoughts of this arrest remain with me today.

Years and years later, when President Nixon's associates broke into the Watergate Towers, it reminded me of that high school experience. He was not anywhere near the Watergate break-in and yet had to resign from office for the actions of someone else.

A few years down the road, I bought and became the owner of a small neighborhood liquor store on Cooper Street. In the store I kept a Miranda camera. A 35-mm Japanese single-lens-reflex model that I kept up on a shelf. One night, the store was broken into and the thief or thieves took that camera. It was a short time after the camera went missing that the police were reciting suspects of their Miranda Rights. Mellissa Rivers later named her son Cooper.

After the passing of my grandfather, my grandmother couldn't keep up with the farm work and decided to sell the property. While it was on the market, my friends would come to visit the farm on weekends. Our parties were initially small gatherings for a few, but they soon escalated into a weekend parties for many, including quite a few strange party-crashers. People were dancing in the kitchen, urinating in the cow trough in the barn. Cars were parked in the driveway, on the highway, and in fields. Things became out of control, and I had to tell my father and ask him what to do about the situation. He took control and was able to put a stop to the weekend parties. I must admit that was a fun time! A short while later, in the late sixties, people gathered at a farm in Woodstock, NY for a very famous three-day festival.

In the late fifties, the parents of my girlfriend Phyllis bought a Castro Convertible couch, the kind that opened up into a guest bed. Soon after that, Fidel Castro overthrew the Fulgencia Batista regime in Cuba and appointed himself, Castro, as the country's dictator.

Phyllis lived in a rural area. Her neighbor's name was Bradley. Coincidentally, in the early sixties, a Princeton basketball forward named Bill Bradley became a star. Playing forward, he earned a gold medal with the 1964 Olympic team as an amateur, and then led Princeton to a third-place finish in the 1965 NCAA Championships— an astonishingly high mark for an Ivy League school. Bradley went on to become a Rhodes Scholar, played professionally with the New York Knickerbockers where he helped win two championship titles. Knickerbocker beer was always a favorite. After leaving basketball, he was a three-term senator in New Jersey.

Phyllis Monroe and I remained an item and were later married in the early sixties. It was October of 1962, soon after Phyllis Monroe and I were married, that Marilyn Monroe died mysteriously in Brentwood, California. Her death was immediately labeled a suicide, but many conspiracy theorists—including the novelist Norman Mailer—has claimed that CIA operatives killed her because they wanted to keep secret her alleged affairs with both John Kennedy and his brother Bobby.

While Phyllis and I were initially seeing each other, long before our marriage, we sometimes had our disagreements and would go our separate ways for a while. There was a time when some friends of mine gathered, and we took a trip to a beach in Rhode Island. While at the beach, I met a girl who was attending the College of New Rochelle in New York. She was kind of cute, and while we were having a nice conversation and drinking a beer, Phyllis suddenly appeared, immediately coming up to us and asking me some heated questions. I stood up and tried to talk to her. She was angry and grabbed my shirt. She ripped the shirt and a couple of buttons ripped off as a result, she then left with her girlfriend. Soon after that, everyone was talking about being "ripped off," a slang expression for being deceived or getting robbed.

While we were still in high school, a girl named Sherri was often seen wandering the halls in an attention-getting red dress. She was a friend of Phyllis and lived nearby. Soon after we graduated high school in the early sixties, Frankie Valli had a hit record "Sherri." Valli's music is still linked in my mind with those times. I was on my way to becoming an adult, and my father often told me to "Walk Like a Man." Phyllis at times would wear a wrinkled sweater. She was a "Rag Doll."

My brother, Michael, has his own musical contribution to this history. He and I once commandeered a rowboat that was tied along the shoreline of a river; we rowed it across the river and tied it on the other side. Then we hiked through the woods to a local airport. Of course, when we returned, the boat was gone. We had to hike a half- mile downstream to where the river was shallow and cross at that point. After our experience with the disappearing boat, the folk gospel song "Michael, Row the Boat Ashore" was made famous by the Highwaymen.

My sister Alyce often called me Jackson, and after a while, well, Michael Jackson separated from the Jackson Five and became a big star.

The movie *Alice Doesn't Live Here* Anymore is reminiscent of my sister Alyce. She had recently been married. While my mother was living with my younger sister, Aileen, mother was always talking about Alyce. Finally, Aileen had to tell mother, "Alyce doesn't live here anymore."

It was about this same time or shortly after that we rented an apartment nearby. After a while, we welcomed our new daughter. Meanwhile, the couple living upstairs also had a baby. They named the baby Caroline. While the baby was still in diapers, Neil Diamond sang his hit song "Sweet Caroline."

While we were taking care of our new addition, my wife's sister met a hippie fellow. Drugs were being used more often and they became good friends and after a few years, in the late sixties, they were married. They married in a park and many guests arrived without shoes or were wearing sandals, had long hair and dresses down to their ankles. I must not forget the German Shepard dog. After the wedding in the park, Neil Simon produced a play called *Barefoot in the Park*.

Dion and the Belmonts were a top group in the late fifties and early sixties. It was in the early sixties that Dion DiMucci went on his own. Frankie Valli and the Four Seasons were also leading the charts in the early sixties with many songs in the Top Ten. In the later sixties, the group experienced major personal changes.

Once Phyllis and I were married, it seemed as though the music itself was beginning to change. In the early seventies, Don McLean sang "American Pie," a song about disillusionment. Its key line was "the day the music died." In one of the verses, the singer said "Drove my Chevy to the levee, but the levee was dry."

In the town of Mansfield where we lived, there was a dam, and stretching out from it was a levee, built by the Army Corps of Engineers, that went quite a distance. The purpose of the levee was to protect the area from flooding. It was always dry and the area never flooded. We would drive to the levee, park the car, and sit listening to the car radio. I also realize the song was a tribute to Buddy Holly who died in a plane crash twelve years earlier.

In the mid-seventies, I bought a new Oldsmobile. I ordered special tags that read JCT-1. Whenever the car was parked at a mall or supermarket, people would ask me where Highway 1 was. I had to explain that the plate wasn't referring to an intersection with a road: It was simply my initials plus the number one.

Later, Lincoln replaced their Town Car with a sportier model called the MKZ. They also introduced a model called the MKT which happened to be my brother's initials.

When we were kids, we would go to a small town near a river where we would climb up and navigate our way to a cliff that was approximately one hundred yards above a river. We would jump from the cliff into a perfect pool made by the river.

In the Mexican resort town of Acapulco, local men would dive from a cliff at LaQuebrada to entertain tourists with their daring dive from the cliffs. In the seventies, we would travel to Acapulco annually for vacation. It became a wonderful annual event. We went sailfishing, watched the divers, and enjoyed the beautiful sunsets at Pie de la Questa. We would also visit and relax at an open air café in El Centro Acapulco. Our waiter's name was Porfilio. It was a short time later they were singing "Porfilio"

My father heard of, and traveled to see, a little beach town north of Acapulco called Zihuatenajo; he wanted to see what they were building and how they were developing Zihuatanejo. Soon the town became a major resort area on the west coast of Mexico. It was about twenty years later that a movie called The Shawshank Redemption was released starring Morgan Freeman as Red and Tim Robbins as Andy, two guys who escaped from prison and met in Zihuatenejo.

My father eventually opened his own shop. I needed income since we were having another baby and went to work with him. We worked with the research and development department at United Technologies. The place of business was 357 Pleasant Valley Road. Once we sold the business, the .357 pistol became a popular weapon. In the shop, we also worked with oil coolant when grinding metal. The place would get smoky, and by the end of the day, the oil was like grease covering our skin. It was in the early seventies that a musical called Grease, directed by Thomas Kail, was presented on Broadway. Grease was the Broadway show that finally broke the record for continuous performances that had been set ten years or so earlier by Fiddler on the Roof. Grease later became a movie starring John Travolta and Olivia Newton John.

On my way home from work, I would often stop at the corner, 7-Eleven and buy some candy for the kids. Of course, they were happy to see me and began jumping with joy. A short time later, Sammy Davis Jr. had a big hit, quite possibly the biggest of his long career, with "Candy Man".

Later in the 1970s my father passed away, and around that time, Phyllis, my wife, was seeing another fellow. That eventually spelled the end of our marriage.

We parted ways and Kenny Rogers began singing a song called "You Picked a Fine Time to Leave Me Lucille." "With four hungry children and a crop in the field, I've had some bad times, lived through some sad times. But this time. . ." And yes, Phyllis and I had four kids, and it was a sad time for this fellow.

Her husband died of cardiac arrest after a short marriage to Phyllis.

Very recently, the singer Billy Paul passed away. In 1972, near the time that Phyllis and I broke up, he enjoyed his biggest chart success of all with a song about a love affair going on outside of a marriage, "Me and Mrs. Jones." Needless to say, that song accentuated emotions that were then very difficult for me to bear. All I had to do was listen to the music and knew what was going on.

It was also in the mid-seventies that I sent a letter to Leslie Stahl of CBS News. She at that time was a reporter for the nightly news with Walter Cronkite. It was a complimentary letter telling her what a great job she was doing and to keep up the good work. It was about a week and a half later that she had written back. She said, thank you for the nice letter and to keep watching CBS News. After we exchanged letters, a fellow by the name of Letterman appeared on the Tonight Show with Johnny Carson and, of course, as they say, the rest is history.

When my wife and I divorced she found another fellow, it was time to sell the house, liquidate, and make plans for a different lifestyle. This was not easy since I truly loved Phyllis and never married again. After we made plans to sell the house, I bought a one-way ticket to Acapulco. While I was on extended vacation there, a girl named Jane appeared, and the two of us became friends. She was a student at UCLA, and we stayed at a condo with a scenic view of Acapulco Bay. Before we moved into the condo, she was staying downtown at a hotel called Hotel California.

While in Acapulco, I called home one day to see how the settlement went with the sale of the house. Phyllis claimed the new owners kept the washer and dryer. Now it was time to return home and reclaim the appliances. Shortly after my return home, the Eagles were singing a song on the radio called "Hotel California."

I never returned to Mexico. Instead, I went to Atlantic City once my gaming license was approved and worked in a casino called Bally's during the week. On weekends, I worked at the Golden Nugget in the limousine department. Steve Wynne was in control at the Nugget.

While at the Nugget, I obtained an upgrade with my gaming license. I had never played the game of craps and thought it would be a good learning experience and challenge. I was awarded my license to deal craps but never had a chance to work as a dealer in a casino. Instead, the limousine position kept me busy. When entertainer Frank Sinatra would come to town, most of the fleet was in New York City. I was often sent to Staten Island, and I transported many mob people. They were heavy tippers and would often make my day.

One time, they sent me to Manhattan to drop off some guests. Once the guests departed, I parked the limo on Third Avenue between forty- sixth and forty-seventh Streets, went to a deli, bought a sandwich, and sat watching the news on TV in the back of the limo. Suddenly, a flash came on the news. A shooting had just taken place at Stark's Steakhouse on forty-sixth Street, just around the corner from where I was parked. I locked up the car and walked a half block to forty-sixth to where I saw sharpshooters on top of buildings and a body on the sidewalk. It was "Tall Paul" Castellano, and his driver, Thomas Bilotti, was in the middle of the street and "Tall Paul" was on the sidewalk. I had never seen anything like this and was totally frightened. I quickly returned to the limo and very soon I was on the New Jersey Turnpike heading south. Those days were always exciting. Once in a while, they were a little too exciting. After a period of time, it was determined that John Gotti was responsible for the shooting.

There was also a time when they needed a car at the thirty-forth Street heliport on the east side to meet Steve Wynne and his guests. They dispatched my car, and I met the driver from the corporate office located on Park Ave. Once the helicopter arrived, Steve Wynne and his wife Elaine appeared. Behind Steve and Elaine were Frank Sinatra and his wife Barbara. When I saw them, I simply panicked. They wanted to go to the Waldorf, and there was some construction on Park Avenue. I turned to the other driver and asked for some ideas. This took maybe a couple of minutes until Sinatra jumped from the back seat and told us to get moving, since they were late for dinner. I thought I would fall over. However, we made it to the Waldorf, on time, without incident.

It was summertime in the early eighties, and I was in the limo without passengers in Manhattan. I took a drive downtown to Houston Street and went into Katz's Delicatessen. There, I ordered a corned beef sandwich on rye bread and a cup of coffee. The sandwich was too big and wrapped half of it to take home. It was a short time after the stop at Katz's Deli that the Tony Award-winning musical Cats began selling out on Broadway. It ran for eighteen years, establishing yet another new record for longevity on the Great White Way.

Aunt Jo-Anne died in 2003 at the age of eighty-three. Her funeral and viewing were held in Connecticut. She was a great person who never drank or touched a cigarette. I loved to be with aunt Jo-Anne. She always made me feel comfortable when I came to visit. She and uncle Nick were always having fun.

After the funeral service, her grandson, who was a bus driver, leased a bus for the day and drove all the funeral guests to the cemetery in Brooklyn, NY where Jo-Anne was to be buried next to uncle Nick who passed a few years earlier. My aunt's casket was placed under the bus while the undertaker rode the bus with everyone else. Once the funeral was over, I started to notice that when someone was not protecting someone or "throwing someone under the bus" was becoming a popular phrase.

Jo-Anne's son, whose name was Len, had a garage on my aunt's property where he built and restored cars and trucks. When Jay Leno took over the Tonight Show, he also became famous for his hobby of rebuilding and selling vintage cars.

When I purchased a liquor store on Cooper Street in a neighboring town the distributors were always producing new products, and one item was a Krackling Rose' wine. In the early seventies, Neil Diamond had a hit song called "Crackling Rosie" which was about loving "a store-bought woman."

A short time later, BMW created a sporty economical little car called a Mini Cooper. Joan Rivers' grandson was also named Cooper. In the early seventies, a thief who called himself D. B. Cooper jumped from an airplane with a large sum of money, estimated at $200,000.00. To this day D.B. Cooper has not been found. The F.B.I. thinks his real name is McCoy.

In the early seventies, we went to see a Saul Hurok dance production at the Metropolitan Opera. The old Metropolitan Opera House was a beautiful structure on Fortieth Street and Broadway. The "Met" as it was known was torn down one year after we saw the show. The Met moved to its new location "sixty-fifth Street at Lincoln Center on the west side of Manhattan.

When my father was living in an apartment by himself, his brother Bill lost his wife to cancer. Bill moved from Hempstead, Long Island to Connecticut in order to share the apartment and live with my father. In the late sixties, Neil Simon produced a play called The Odd Couple, which was so popular that it spun off into a movie and then a long-running TV show.

When we were young and we had to urinate, our parental instructions were "Go to the bathroom and make a river". I supposed they were being creative. In the mid 1950s, the comedian Joan Molinsky took her stage name as Joan Rivers. One night when I returned home from my bowling league, Joan Rivers was hosting The Tonight Show. I found the show entertaining and became perhaps a little overly fond of the host—in thought anyway. We always had a thoughtful connection after that. Her husband Edgar was in Philadelphia and committed suicide, sadly and for reasons we will never know.

Years later, while preparing for an endoscopy, Joan Rivers was administered the sedative propofol and passed away from cardiac arrest.

When my aunt Sally relocated her daughter from New York to Arizona to attend the University of Arizona in the mid-sixties, Glen Campbell was singing a tune called "By the Time I Get to Phoenix."

One day in February in the early eighties, I went to Washington, DC for a couple of days—mostly to visit Georgetown, and maybe see a ball game at the university. I stayed at the Hilton and when I checked in. I paid cash for the room. Of course. the receipt was misplaced or lost and when I returned home a bill arrived for the cost of the room. I couldn't find the receipt and had to send a check. I called the hotel and tried to explain that the room had already been paid for with cash. They talked to the desk clerk who told them he thought I was giving him a tip. Did that ever make me angry! A couple of weeks after that, President Reagan was to give a talk at the same Hilton hotel. It was then that the president and two others were shot by John Hinckley while leaving the hotel.

In the late nineties, I decided to work on a pilot's license, reasoning that I would save a lot of time whenever I traveled from South Jersey to Connecticut. However, it didn't work out that way. I bought a Piper Cherokee 140 and began working on my pilot's license. One requirement was to fly solo to Salisbury, Maryland. The flight to Maryland was just fine, but on the return trip, I missed a VOR (Very high frequency Omnidirectional Range) signal—a communication system that lets you know if you are on course. I missed the VOR and was headed toward Philadelphia International Airport. Realizing my error, I lowered my altitude and was "flying under the radar" of "class A" airspace. I continued flying east toward the South Jersey shore, flew another thirty minutes, and found my way home.

It was during this flying experience that John Kennedy Jr., flying less than a hundred miles north of me, met his death. He had purchased a Piper Sarasota in the late nineties and was flying it in order to attend a wedding on Martha's Vineyard. He became disoriented due to bad weather and went into the Atlantic Ocean.

In March 2000 another unsettling incident occurred while I was flying with my instructor and her husband from South Jersey to Connecticut. I wanted to visit my kids for a few days. The flight north was without incident, and we assembled a few days later for the return trip. We left Connecticut and flew toward Westchester, New York. We then followed the Hudson River, and when we were at the lower part of Manhattan, my instructor told me to look to the left. I looked over and saw, with some alarm, that the World Trade Center was within a few hundred feet. We were closer than we were supposed to be, but it was a beautiful sight. It was almost a year later that some terrorists from the middle east flew and commandeered airliners into the twin towers known as the World Trade Center.

We were building a house in West Atlantic City at the time and were only a few miles from Atlantic City International Airport. There was no television at the house we were working on and while listening to the radio the news was being broadcast that an airplane crashed into the World Trade Center in New York City. All flights were to land due to a terrorist threat. I ran outside and saw airplanes circling and landing at Atlantic City International. The airport was also a backup landing area for the space shuttle. Of course, no one fully knew why the planes were landing or what was happening until a few hours later when we learned what was happening in New York City.

I often used to tell an airplane joke about a passenger jet traveling to Heathrow from New York when it lost power in one of the engines. They continued flying, but then the other engines began to lose power. The pilot landed the plane in the Atlantic and told the passengers he would continue to call for help and that they should wait for further instructions. A period of ten minutes went by, and the plane began taking in water. The pilot took the microphone again. He explained to the passengers that there was no help in sight. He then told the passengers who knew how to swim to climb out on the right wing while those who couldn't swim could climb out on the left wing and wait again for further instructions. Minutes went by, and there was still no response to the radioed calls for help. The plane began to sink. The pilot grabbed the intercom and said, "Passengers on the right wing who know how to swim please start swimming now. Those on the left wing, who can't swim, thank you for flying Lufthansa." I stopped telling that story in 2009 when Captain "Sully" Sullenberger's Airbus A320 hit a flock of Canadian geese, and he somehow landed the airplane safely in the Hudson River. Fortunately, no one was hurt. People were out on the wings waiting for help.

My mother was also a great pretender. She was always pretending things were going well when they were not. The only time she seemed truly happy was when we would do a road trip or go on vacation. Yes, the Platters' song "The Great Pretender" was exactly the way mother was.

A girl named Sheila would often go with me to sock hops and dance. We were together for a couple of years, and then we went our own way. A short time after our separation, the Platters were singing a song called "Smoke Gets in Your Eyes." The Platters' song perfectly expressed how I felt about losing Sheila. It was Tommy Roe who had a hit called "Sheila" a while after our departure.

The Beach Boys recorded a sweet but pensive song, "In My Room," about needing from time to time to have a safe place to retreat from the world. Brian Wilson, the songwriter and musical genius of the group, went through some serious depression. "In My Room" reflected that. Pretty recently, a terrifically and thoughtfully made movie called Love and Mercy documented the arc of Brian's illness and eventual recovery. After my wife and I sold the house, this writer was experiencing the same emotional situation. I rented a room after divorcing Phyllis and would often just sit alone, looking out the window.

As Operation Desert Storm was reaching its climax, with Scud missiles flying all over the place, and Saddam Hussein's Iraqi troops hightailing it away from their invasion of Kuwait, I always wondered why President George H. W. Bush Sr. didn't seize such a great opportunity to take Saddam Hussein out and have the dictator punished. I remember this every time I think of Sodom, which is the name of a section of the town in Connecticut where we lived, another community near Mansfield. It wasn't until George W. Bush became president that Saddam Hussein was found. He was put on trial and then died while in prison.

When Phyllis was diagnosed with cancer in 2011, it was a tremendous shock. She had always been there to take care of the kids. One of our daughters was disabled, and I traveled back and forth from New Jersey to visit and be with her. Phyllis died soon after that diagnosis, and our daughters were without a mother. They were devastated. It became necessary to moved back to Connecticut in 2012 and tried to fill in for their mother. I had a two-family investment property and made my home in one of the apartments.

After moving from New Jersey to Connecticut that same year, in October, Hurricane Sandy hit the northeastern seaboard states. It was one of the most destructive hurricanes in history, tearing up boardwalks in New Jersey and flooding many coastal towns. Of course, New Orleans was also devastated by the storm. Once again, it was that trail that was left behind.

With four young children my friends often called me papa John. In the year 2016, the Denver Broncos won the Super Bowl. Peyton Manning, quarterback for the Broncos, was always advertising "Papa John's" pizza. Peyton Manning always seemed to enjoy saying and doing funny things.

Now it seems to be that Donald Trump is the main character on the political scene. In the early seventies, my wife and I enjoyed playing bridge with another couple who lived nearby. She was good at playing the hand while my strength was winning the bid. It had been many years since we played, and the "trump" suit was the one played to win the game.

We did many cruises with Norwegian Cruise Line and hold Latitudes Cards for the cruises we did. They can be presented for many discounts when on board. Since we've done these cruises, a bright senator from Texas has appeared, and for quite a while, he was also a contender for the Republican nomination. His name, of course, is Ted Cruz. But his ethnic heritage is more Cuban than Norwegian, I suspect. And he has boldly gambled his political future by refusing to back Trump while running on the Republican ticket. You might even say that, for Trump, Cruz turned himself into a cruise missile. Senator Cruz has since reconciled with Donald Trump.

In 1970, My father adopted Keesh, a Keeshond dog, from Sally, his sister. Wasn't long after when everyone seemed to be eating quiche, a French tart that became popular at favorite eating places.

June 2017. Brother put his condo on the market for sale. The place was put under contract and sold. Before settlement the buyers hired an inspector to see if there were any deficiencies.

The inspector found a crack in the concrete two properties from his condo. The inspector called it crumbling concrete. This report was devastating for my brother and his wife and prompted the buyers to cancel the contract of sale. On June 14, 2017 an unhappy home inspector from Illinois started shooting at republican senators practicing baseball. Representative Scalise and others were wounded after the inspector fired many shots from the screen behind home plate. Senator Scalise has since recovered and is doing well.

It was August 23, 2017 While visiting Sunny in New Jersey and her son walked in. He wouldn't stop talking when I used the word hurricane while talking about the weather. Well, the next week there appeared a hurricane named Harvey.

Harvey was the most destructive storm ever to hit the Texas coast dropping more than thirty inches of rain. There were two highs further north preventing the storm from moving. The rain continued for four days creating massive flooding in the Rockport area, then moving toward Houston and then Louisiana.

When travelling and visiting Alaska a hat bearing the state's name wound up on this writer's head.

Wore the hat while in Connecticut and suddenly the temperature began to drop. The high temperature one day during the week of January 7th was only five degrees. Talked to my sister in New Hampshire and the high was five degrees below zero.

In August of 2017, while driving to New Jersey a pain in my chest appeared. Pulled over on the Turnpike and stopped at the next rest stop. Took a short walk, burped a couple of times and the pain seemed to disappear. It started again while visiting Sunny, my long time friend and the pain started again. Finally at three o'clock in the morning I decided to go to the hospital. They took me in immediately and was told the problem was a hiatal hernia. After two days this patient was transported to Lourdes cardiac center in Camden, New Jersey. They placed a stent in some artery and had to stay overnight. The next day I was sent home. The doctor prescribed three medications that had different side affects. After a while a serious case of diarrhia developed. Made an appointment with my primary care physician and was told to call the heart doctor. Couldn't see the heart doctor until January. Until then I couldn't leave the house for any extended period of time.

In Santa Barbara, California there were heavy mudslides after six inches of rain fell. All in a short period of time.

In February of 2018, my friend Gigi and I went to see the Harry Connick show on fifty-seventh Street in Manhattan. He had several nice people on the show including the wife of Howard Stern. It was in the first part of February and just a couple of weeks after we saw the show "the Harry Connick" show, the show was cancelled.

Was having trouble with a cough. Coughed during the day and at night. Never go to the hospital for any treatment, however, on Saturday(2/10/18) I went to the ER at the local hospital and they gave me some medication for the cough. The medicine worked and eventually the cough stopped.

The following week a twenty-seven year old fellow intentionally crashed his vehicle into the entrance of the Emergency room at the Hospital and then set himself on fire. He was transported to Bridgeport burn center and received the necessary treatment for the burns on his body and some mental treatment.

In November of 2019 Donald Trump was trying to remain president. He had a name for everyone,

Chuck Schumer was called crying Chuck, Michael Bloomberg was called "Little Michael", Nancy Pelosi was "Nervous Nancy", Joe Biden was "sleepy Joe". Then Adam Shiff was a manager and according to Trump, he was "Shifty Shiff". Later in the month a whisleblower appeared. He was a" fraud". He was Ukrainian and the government was trying to find some "quid pro quo" activity". Trump called this "whistleblower" a fraud. He first accused the Russians of being involved and then it switched to Ukrainian involvement. My grandparents were from the Ukraine and it sure looked as though they were looking for me and calling me a "whistleblower"

JANUARY 26, 2020 An awful helicopter accident took place. Kobe Bryant his daughter and seven others were killed in a helicopter crash when they left the city of Calabasas.

The aircraft belonged to Kobe and the pilot was told not to fly due to bad weather. All other aircraft were grounded and they decided to fly. When they left in the morning with dense fog. His daughter was called Gigi and my friend Georgine was also called Gigi. Kobe played high school ball at Lower Marion Township High school. Near Ardmore and just outside Philadelphia. He was in contact with Gino Auriemma and wanted his daughter Gigi to play basketball at the University of Connecticut.

Made plans in February with Norwegian Cruise Lines to take a trip to the Western Caribbean. We made plans to travel to Belize, Roatan and a few other ports of call. We then made airline reservations to fly to Florida. Suddenly, an outbreak of covid 19 virus broke out. The outbreak originated at Wuhan(population 11,000,000) Institute of Virology in China. Conspiracy theorists assumed the lab was the origin of the Covid-19 virus and had spread to Italy and other parts of the world. Now in March 2020 the virus is found on cruise ships. People are being detained on ships for a period of time until everything was cleared on board. Once cleared from the ship those people were quarantined for two days. Later Norwegian Cruise Lines cancelled the cruise

Presidential election day is Nov. 3, 2020. Donald is not that well liked and the stock market is tanking for two weeks before the election. Oct 28, 2020 the market dropped over nine hundred points. All this, so Donald Trump cannot say how wonderful the economy is doing.

Jimmie Smith now lives in a town called Surfside Beach, So Carolina. He had been using my identification to obtain his driver's license since his license was revoked in the state of New Jersey and he moved to South Carolina.

Another awful coincident occurred in Surfside area of Miami Beach July, 2021 when a condominium building collapsed. A cruel legacy that left a total of 97 lives lost. The reason for the collapse is unknown.

Just another coincident when the clock on the wall of my bedroom makes a tic-toc sound. That sound keeps this fellow's thought process tuned to the tic-toc when there is too much to think about. The next thing was an app found on the telephone and became popular called tic-toc.

It's now December 23, 2021 and a tenant who lives upstairs with a son who is seven years old and a daughter a bit older. Her age is thirteen and her name is Valentina. A tragic shooting took place in Los Angeles when a girl who was fourteen years old, in a dressing room, was shot and killed by a policeman when the bullet went through a wall in the dressing room. Her name was also Valentina.

Printed in the United States
by Baker & Taylor Publisher Services